D1289702

BIRTH OF A SHARK

Birth
of
a
Shark

POEMS
BY
DAVID WEVILL

MACMILLAN
London · Melbourne · Toronto

ST MARTIN'S PRESS
New York
1966

© David Wevill 1964

First Edition 1964
Reprinted 1966

MACMILLAN AND COMPANY LIMITED
Little Essex Street London WC 2
also Bombay Calcutta Madras Melbourne Sydney

THE MACMILLAN COMPANY OF CANADA LIMITED
70 Bond Street Toronto 2

ST MARTIN'S PRESS INC
175 Fifth Avenue New York NY 10010

PRINTED IN GREAT BRITAIN

For Assia

Acknowledgments

THE author is grateful to Penguin Books Ltd. and to the Oxford University Press for permission to reprint poems which first appeared in *Penguin Modern Poets 4* and *A Group Anthology*. Acknowledgments are also due to the B.B.C. quarterly programme, 'The Poet's Voice', and to the Editors of *Ambit, The Chelsea, The Critical Quarterly, Developmental Medicine and Child Neurology, The Listener, The Massachusetts Review, The New Yorker, The New York Times, The Observer,* and *The Sewanee Review.*

Contents

My Father Sleeps

WHO brought from the snow-wrecked
Hulk of winter his salvaged
Purpose ; who came, blind but friendly
By these lines his mouth and his eyes
Have fixed ; and without further talk
Taught me at last how to walk,
Until by his power I came
Out of innocence like the worm's flame
Into daylight. What practical need
His patience had, and anger bred
Of disillusionment, has gone with age.
I have this white-haired image,
Arrogant perhaps, and too much the hero
For our friendship's good : Lear, although
Afraid of words as of madness,
Of procrastination as of disease —
A lover of plain-spokenness —
Though not where it hurt, that he could understand.
If I trace the scars in my right hand
They tell me of purpose disobeyed,
Of old and factual truths my head
Cannot alter. And watching him thus
Sprawled like a crooked frame of clothes
In the sleep of sixty years, jaws firm,
Breathing through the obstacle of his nose
A stubborn air that is truth for him,
I confront my plainest self. And feel
In the slow hardening of my bones, a questioning
Depth that his pride could never reveal ;
That in his sleep stirs its cruel beginning.

At Rideau Falls

THE tideless Ottawa is small
Beside the rivers of old capitals ;
Is logged by nylon-shirted men,
Match-makers. At Rideau Falls
I watch, drunk, the thrust of a barge
Bruising my ribs with each lurch, coils
Of surf stampeding up the night.
I will not come back. My time
Outlingers cities ; my warm children
Rest surly in my head. They will own
This germ of me that failed to grow.
They will pick stark fables from my bones.

Spiders

MUDDLING up the wooden stairs one night, in my socks
Past screens and shuttered bunting-creviced wallboards,
My tongue dry, but a cool wind puffing thinly soft
Up my torn shirt-front, the dust hot-thick in my hair,
I crossed my sister coming that way in her slip —
The steep way down, half-asleep ; her chicken-hearted breathing
And toes antennaed for spiders or bits of fluff
That might jiggle and spill a mouse. I tasted my own breath
Kekking, milkweed-sour, after the beer —
But not to budge, or her shriek might wake the house —
Who is it ? I didn't know her face —
Such full pails for eyes ! she might have been glass ;
The roman nose, pink lips peeled white over salt
While ten years woke up and started. . . . I thought myself
Back, a loiterer in jeans, hands spittled with oil
From throbbing handlebars. Wind shoulders the porch,
Flickers the close trees. . . . I held back then
And jammed my buttocks hard against black wood,
My back a prickly heat of rusty nails which
Builders'd slapped in, and left, when the lake was young
With all her forests open to the wind, mated conifers
Exploding dry cones. I listened in the dark,
And thought, this wife won't wait to be woken by me,
But go on down, passing me, always on my left —
Wind clacking the picture-frames through our big house —
I wasn't going to wake her. I mightn't have seemed
Her brother, then, but eight legs sprung on her dream,
Something she'd sense far worse than spiders, on the stair,
That could harm her children. Maybe it wasn't just fear,
Or concern, that made me cringe from her.
Two people who cross in the dark walk nearest to ghosts,
Her terror might have stuck its mouth in me,
And sealed her against a love she could not cope with,
Grinning under heavy sheets, with her heartbeat.

3

Elegy for a Live Brother

Now I am ten years older, almost nine
For your birthdays come between, and I've known
October go smoking out without my remembering.

It is a long disease, this lapse of brothers

A distance guessed in years.   One can be morbid
Thinking back ; the blushing acne and the sore crotch —
Always too well dissembled to discover
From what indolence, or fault of good behaviour
Your head scans brother's habits for tidemarks now,
Unwilling to kick a conventional breeding from the mouth,
To shock those seemly wardens, and proud Pastor Crouch . . .

Hasty notes are harder to write than that . . .

There is this photograph : doll-mechanism of a smile,
Stretched taut between pegs, like underwear on a line ;
Face beetling into the sun : 'Your brother is
Half an inch shorter than dad . . .'   That's six foot two ;

And in the new car's polished, sky-streaked doors,
Your length loops and skips like a flapping
Banner above parades !   But is it all
Smooth tan and teeth, a smile round as an apple,
Or is there some way young brothers inherit
Old flaws from hand-me-downs ; a hat or a shoe
Infects ; and only the bones outgrow and grow ?

I know my dry stone is lodged in your brain.

Somehow there must be a room where we can meet,
Somewhere, cramped, with a naked drop of light fixed
Shivering up there, above our eyes, to smash . . .
Lidless . . . to crash like tears our eyes dismiss . . .

4

But not that cast-off shell of a house on the long beach,
That empty beach where only you belong,
The sandy riddles and porcelain stones each
Summer my heels indented, bled when spiked by glass —

I will not apologize. My comfortable mockeries burst
Blood at your open ear, brushed that wide grin with stones ;
I battled against your growing, hated your growing,
Wanting it all to be ache and scrape, that I'd console,

Desiring it hard for you, so I could pity.

In Love

SHE touches me. Her fingers nibble gently.
The whole street leans closer, its doors
Grin open and cluster shut,
Gathering like a fist closing, firmly.
Warm Sunday mornings breathe a way of knowing
God's love, his shuddering mouth to mouth
Vision above the brain's heat,
Beyond leather foot, bible, or prayer book —
Naked we push their webbed stares out.

Look, bodies that puzzled me no longer love ;
Effulgence of grasses cover her body —
I champ and am at sea and drown and feed,
Hurl and kiss, climb and descend,
Lie still with the prickle of ants underneath me.
There was an opening, an opening —
It's gone now. Now there's no question of fire,
Grasses, or drowning ; only this first
Dry building of rib above rib, as if
A great house crumbled on its skeleton.

And this is my Sunday lesson she teaches me.
Her texts are pillows, strong wrists and liquid ankles.
I could paint her as I fell on her,
And did, with my tongue, lungs and my whole heart,
Each breath exploding its hot ether lash
Through our wills to their blind core.
If this is love I grieve for God's —
His idolators shuffling by with their scrubbed
        children ;
Though her face, with its sky-change coloured eyes,
Melts them all one in my privilege.

6

Body of a Rook

GOD broke upon this upturned field ; trees
Wedged tangled and thick as black crotch-hair —
But an eyelid in the field's face flutters,
Winks, blindingly. Whose
Sunrise through that blazing shrub glows
Ram's horns ? twin forks of a tree,
Dividing, splitting. And nothing disturbs
These soft tussocks, the woman's one-eyed love.

In the scenery of crushed glass, here,
Among kneading hands of mud, the scoured head lies,
A world seized between sunlit clouds,
Spinning with sense, one eye gone black.
I stare out over my roof of towns,
And shiver off my sperm of wet dog-hair —

Night's claw, where cats couple among
The strict soldiering lupins. As afterthoughts,
My manners brush their teeth into the sink ;
A cloud keeps my bed, the hot patch kept,
Warmth of armpits and incendiary struggles —
I return where my love gloats and swarms to sleep.

Imagine, if our naked bones
Broke up on these same stones, that freed stubble
Mouth jagged as smashed plastic —
Our nakedness breathes and shifts through warm holes,
Sighs from pricked gaps (the manners torn) ;
We know our natures and our flaws
Closer, from such uncharitable hunting . . .

I prise the blue-black feathers back. The beak glows,
Soft at the edges, like an urchin's valve-
Mouth. I know my own violence too.

7

I feel her gnawing, clinging, flesh-stubbed
Teeth in me, my remembrance of her mouth.
It is a killing but who dies ?

I killed it slowly with a lump of flint.
Shot down and left to die, what soft thing jerks
Its pulped head, face, body, nerves
Beak-deep in the pasture mud ? I watched
Those last sufferings leave her body too,
Twitching black and rook-supple before
I kicked my damaged violence into the wood.

Poem

I AM alone in body :
My love is an outrider
Who scorns my cores of frost,
Wanders south along old lines
With her soul wrapped in furs. . . .
Change is change,
It cannot be forced or adored
For better, for worse.

You walk in loudening circles around me,
Licking the treetop-shattered wind
For empty sustenance.
Your trail is subtle,
And in this cold
No scent carries.

Separation

JETTIES suck, suck.
The broken and muddy water grips
Without purpose. The water has
Nowhere else to go, like ships.

Derricks could be of flesh
But seen through, X-rayed to the bone.
A gaunt skyline geometry,
Abstracts jerking out of human

Eyes a like jaggedness.
I imagine I see you borne
Bobbing on the brown water,
Your round eyes grey under the cold horn

Of the fog. And I touch
The river as if skin met skin,
A body identified
But crabbed, gelid, a frayed fraction,

A hermit grip rising out of the mud.
The parcel of sky, crammed, undelivered
Rains. All across the water
Tugs steam like burning dead.

In an instant the flayed river
Hisses up to the jetties
Crawling as if on legs. The ridge
Of that far bank disappears.

The river's itself. Your head
Bending down over the lettered keys
In your factory-loud office, feels
The waters surge back. You close your eyes.

Germinal

WASTES grow ; you lean into the sun
As towards a good husband, hoping its fire
Will incinerate your trash and not you.

Above us the dogged stars sweat and freeze,
Mimicking suns. Who can they be,
These germless, clean immortals ?
They suffer laws beyond our laws —

Strictures, paradox. Devils play
In the hair of the hillside, if you look too close.

The sun seeps into and through your bones,
Flushing the clotted soil,
Tapping bacteria, mites, and the locked
Purses of beetles. And you, fiery and whole

Are pure waste matter, aged to a diamond's strength ;
Your will and body, stone and root,
Mind playing the manager, body the staff
That bears it.

                        — Listen to me now ;
I bring my life to you, like a petition
Expecting an answer. Heart and heart,
Beating in the one way of hearts,
Earthward, my founding engine.

Under the slipshod leaves beaten to leather
With the thawing March rain, relaxed
As only the warmth and wet can relax —
Fur, nails, sinuses, muscles —
Don't choose your first-found patch of bones
For the coffin of our vows.

I feed on your wastes, as nothing can on perfection
But must starve, or go bad
In its own time, so brimming with its death.

Let me carry your wastes through my mouth,
Carefully, as a cat lifts its young ;
Or better, as a she-goat eats her afterbirth,

Assuming to herself her rightful body,
Without regret or distaste,
Certain of her ways, if not their names.

Fraying-Stocks

I AM tall as this ruined tower
Or short as this grassblade. Travelling the sun's
Arc, I am neither.
Just my shadow changing height with the day.

I have witnesses. The falcon,
The May-beetle's grubs ; these,
And the thumping feet of dancers have broken me open.

Walking between trees, hawthorn
And elm in an April downpour, I grow
A black glistening coat of bark —
No disguise but a kind of touch ;
My rings of parsnip iron
Could be mistaken for grief around the eyes.

Soon, when the weather breaks
I'll go. Already the sap pushes a hard
Corolla of nails over my flowering jaws.
Face of hectic white —

Blood familiar to blackflies —

The treacherous nearness of life
Under surfaces trained to hold and protect,
Embarrassed by the green eyes of ponds,
Outstares the clocks of cities, —

A ritual sickness grows
In the antler's shape ; breaks with my flight ;
But is cured by no
Thoughts of returning, no hope of change.

Hysteria

QUEER, straining life. Her perfect
Anatomy, puzzled even at birth
When closest to a simple trust in stars, —
Now crushed in a smash-up of steel,
The nerves of experience, helpless as ever, dangling
From one strap of half-
Torn-off ear, lit in the pouring
Headlights of her shock ! In the dead quiet
A little alive. In the unbelievable numbed
Quiet, a fraction better off than dead —
Is this the dream you had to have,
Tugging at the black sleeve of your sleep ?
Coherence and formula, pattern, everything gone.
Here are but ant-bitten heaps ; some struggling queen
Blinded by acid love, and below
The delicate courage of her fiery suitors ;
A meeting-place where all might talk and drink
To danger and hunger, mumbling
Of naked childhood and merged
In blind thoughts of motherhood ; like a millpond teeming
With a liquorice fungus of tadpoles
She is replete . . . full of her past,
As a history scholar. And now, spoiling dream,
Go. Keep close to her side ;
Run with her as your arrows thwack her dazed.
Force her to quench her sight with the way
Her permanent blood leaps to vacate her body —.
Whether virgin or plain woman, the same
Mistrust of giving, waits to be crude-forced.

A Legend

THE sinewy nerves of a cabbage now
Contain my head. Its pulse-count
Falls to a trickle, under the icing of hope.

I am more things than a vegetable,
Or a landscape battered blue by March ;
I run over them. I perpetrate
Cruelties at their roots. And still they follow
Their needs and ways : burns
Heal in the generations, old wounds grow stony
And bother nothing but the mind.

Through it all, my telltale streaks in the wind
From her quarter. I am more
Than these things. Who would judge my secrets ?

So I wake one morning, and tell my legs
Of the difficult journey made
Aghast in the dream. How small I must make myself !
And how great —

With catastrophe ! The beating of rain
Eats into the sun's thaw. I have gathered wood
To build my shadow a fire —
Is she female ? At lunch I chew my meat
Slowly, wondering if I am vegetarian.

I nibble drily at crusts and become
The whole, huskless grain before an aching fire.
A pride like mine must have
More lives in its hands than one,
And in such generous variety that
The stars seem egotistical. Who would complain

Of the number of swordblades and plowblades
Through which the earthworm now
Pushes his waste ? And still

The deserted, the dead, and the blind go underground,
To weep at these monstrous remains
That never grew in them.

I watch them now ;
My altars of fire and sunlight become
Too crowded with worshippers. I go down
Hoping, Eurydice, to find you there.

Valediction

OBSESSION with the dead is a kind of vagrancy.
Tell me what I must do, woman of salt,
To reconvene the birds above our darkness,
The day-lamps and electric stars.

I too am alive ; what properties are gone
From the metal of my glance
To keep you hobbled with this boulder's dead
Weight ? There is no god in the dark —
Dark is mindless, embodied only
By restless, rootless sight.
Dark penetrates into your brain.

The galaxies of blood burn in you like rage.

This is no place to loiter in,
Trapped between the twitching of your hands
And memories of a more violent dark,

The imprisoning 'Yes' and 'No' of your small habits
Hungering for their afterbirths.

The light this black nothing takes is yours —
You have brought it with you, your
Covenant and familiar : here's how life comes fresh
Under the icy rivulet of survival.

This light's your embodying, like a lynx-smell
Where the body crouches, over its tiny fire —

It is a decision, formed, obdurate, hard
Through much enduring, like
The shelved heart of quartz or the fierce
Seizure that stopped the moon.

Take it, it is yours . . .

But even the salt crystals on your skin
Give no answer ; the sense is lost, and the search
Through the dark leads you back
Where your eyes swam to their beginning.

Now trust the light that's there,
Under your frontal bone,
And the flesh, and bring the secret back.
No one can tell any better,
Or dream where that light came from.

This is your birth-spark's only miracle.
It is the unmaimed last moment you will live.

Irish Hotel

THIS is the last hotel
And the last light on the sea.
A mind whitewashed and stripped clean to the salt
Wind : its eyes
Have the narrow watchfulness of the builder,
Wary, because alone. Sleepless, discreet,
Distracted through its panes of diamond lead
The desk-clerk is the sea's proprietor
For a moment. Our entry now
Builds a fire in the grate beneath his stare.

Usually the weather's kinder, he says. But lies,
Believing the rocks out there are moments of sun ;
The lights in his eyes are sea-moons,
They have no pupils. The wind
Has gouged headland and sky
With the lines of his forehead. Deeper inland
Is the time he dreams of : pools of trout,
Hills, a lakebed, castle-ruins and towns.

Better to tell him the wind's blown us here,
Than that we've come
Poring over his stone floors, for a home
Unlike any he knows.
Creation is cold —
His coat of tweed covers difficult bones ;
When bad food and a cold bed
Bring day up over the horizon, the sea
An infinite black still, or a vague puzzle of grey across
His features, he knows
We must leave. Though, for a night
His wet wind grows on us like skins,
And he wouldn't guess our strangers' minds' need
To love his rocks' black bodies,

The iodine of his bruised sand
Spread over the soiled bones of distant farms his mind

Dwells on. If to-morrow's sunrise
Gives us back the world of photographs —
Castles, perfect, and towns teeming with life's
Human mice, — he is not at odds
With our broken beginnings. There,
His roof of shaved black slate,
The diamond-panes of his eyes,
His ankles of thick rough stone, would become
Our hard bed of dreams ; his sea flawless.

August

GRADUALLY the grape
Spins her green blood,
Shares with the apples and pears
Bitterness of a sweet tooth.
This breakfast the sun takes,
Furious fire gorged on green water
Fluent as envy —
Now with some jealousy her vines wait
The heel of the sickle,
Where wood ends and steel finishes,
And flesh ends before wood begins,
And bone before that.   The sun
Pleads no amnesty, but perfects.
A hundred goblins at the foot of a tree
Wither like grapeskins,
And swell like wineskins,
Swimming into summer over our eyelids.
The old man with his sickle,
A lip of rust at the edge,
Is the last to leave the party.

William Blake

THE god-philosopher, the watcher —
His eyes control my nature.
They smother with their meaningless grey stare
The nothing of another person.

The eyes are my prison ; they are my release.
The eyes are what I have made of myself,
They give me facts —
As a man, ten years after a battle,
Remembers it all in false detail.

That stare is my pride.
Through it a sodden, bottom-heavy world
Flashes lightning : the lighthouse glimpsed
Light falls on a sea whose size is calm.

In detail, then ; these scarred, rough
Extremities of hand and foot,
Antennae of the common moth,
Breed true to habit. My eyes tell what
The greater body knows of this —

The watcher is neutral ;
He must be. What he has seen
Has stunned him into being the god he is.
His agony must triumph elsewhere ;
He must live.

Wine-Cask

WHAT is blacker than a black horse,
The coffin seems to ask ;
Unless it is the shadow of this church.
Nothing is blacker than this doorway —
Even in England they can't
Manufacture such a depth of black.
Why must they carry my black oak
Through the sunlight, on their high shoulders.
Why not just let me slip
This bulk loose, and return to the forced root ?
'This contrast', the mourners say,
'Is necessary for our friend's beginning.
He must make a new start —
Patterns on the sand in the sunlight.
Take the brightest and darkest of life
And bury them together.
Meanwhile we wear our mourning
Between dawn and twilight,
Shaved chins and veils over our moles.'

Goya's 'Snowfall'

AT quiet heights where snow is at home
Through four seasons, winter is still the worst.

The cold hills settle, grey on white,
Tracks turn to nothing overnight.

All three abreast and in step, these men
Come shrouded, huddle with their thoughts ;
Their companions come roundabout ; the pack-horse
Churns their tracks, a blaze of sleet
Stitching his eyes.   And theirs

As at a friend's death humbled,
Each figure drags his manhood through
The hearthfire smouldering under his cloak —

The storm-wind hounds them cripple-backed,
The driven snow blows in with bleeding knuckles
Under their grey hoods.   And only

The blizzard lives.   The horse, the men
Endure it, and watch each other ; watch
With that man-striving struck patience that makes
The mountainous cold seem a white ally,
A whispering dread that circles but will not strike.

And under it all, the priest-black sodden ground
Hardens.   What their eyes tell
Is such plain conspiracy : of the fear at their backs
Where the wind turns, sifts, yard above soft yard,
The snow-metallic water smell
Of God's grace and font.

                    Prisoners of snow,
The men come trudging through my burial ground,
Bringing their horse and habits.   And the hills
Spinning like blindness, keep their word,
Follow them to their hearthfires and their graves.

Flying Fish

SWIMS with the long swirl of eels at first ; then
The sharp quick wake, a white scar breaking
Across the wave's side like a cast line. Instinct
Confuses ship's wake with wave, imagining
Rearing walls and valleys past which escape
Teases the knifing fins to wing

From wave-ridge to ridge. The world swims
Through this fish, swells, bursts over his eye
In cold fevers ; subsides. Whole schools may
Scatter away on a fin, leap-frogging the spray
The ship's dead iron plunge throws back like hair.
Sometimes they wait just under a wavehead ; lie

Still and patient as bait, peeldrift ; then suddenly
Across a warm magenta sea the silent
Scream of their flight drums on a wave
That baffles them, feels solid, drives them spent
Downward, or spits them up like rain-beats
Off a pavement. By no accident

Will these fish climb to poison the sea's calm :
Defying the bitter-as-salt air they may dive
Briefly, upward, like Icarus to waylay
The meridian sun ; or they may strive
To outplay some vair-edged shadow that startles them
Fathoms beneath : and swim through air to live.

Water Poem

IN this sea I find a lake,
Its white-ribbed waves and grey deep flesh
Drags skeletons up by the hair,
Every wavelet a luminous eyeball.
For boys who loved water, for men who tear at it
Frenziedly, like a fifth wife,
The sea's salt distils
To birth-freshness. But now, when the wind
Drives down hard, and the big clouds turn and heave
Ploughshares of wet grey over the water,
I see through the salt a clear eye
Closed for ever on a night of deep water —
A man's lungs burst with fresh water,
A man's throat choked with salt.

                              Some body that drowned
Would grow that perpetual lull in its cells,
Sweeping and washing with
The eardrum-poised crayfish : flesh
Discarded, the sea's afterbirth —
Freshwater cells and the salt pores tight
As wet drumskins, unwinding with
The sea's time that unravelled Ahab —
The sea's freshwater diet, men and the rain.

In our childhood there was a lake
That changed its cry three times a day, and the fourth
Time was night. Its deadheads rose up
Erect out of the washlight,
Fertilized dragonflies, stove boat-hulls in.
These were incidentals. We knew
That a lake is as deep as the land around it
Allows : as a man is deep,
But dies to that greater depth, sea and the rain.

26

Pisces

I WALKED over the sand breathing wind,
Alone at that only permitted hour
When the fugitive wears no hood.
Dawn rose ; the south wind would not let go,
And I stood for a while, looking south —
My eyes like leafbuds hadn't yet opened —
I stood, and wondered at nothing at all
But the casualness of my watching the sea
From depths as great as its cancers of live squid,
Sharks, crabs, at that hour too far from the mind's
Whet ; depth too heavy in me to float free.
Here lay scattered, and there, throughout my head
Lives too broken to fight again ;
Exhausted, unforgiving heads,
World-haters of the world that furnished, fed
And crushed them.   They were like a man
Whose crooked eyes betray his grin ;
They were mine, my creatures, stealthily opening.

In a leafbud's tiny complete year,
Its safely-rehearsed beginning and end
The sea has no place.   Its depths divide
In swarming numbers, breed in shoals —
Sea-creatures and men, they wade
Their memories guardedly, with double swords.
But the tides that have wallowed through time
The first queasy jerkings of breath, break
Now, in the windstung half-dark of my brain.
The south wind won't let go —
These broken lives and habits wake and yawn
With the stretching simplicity of cats.
I feed my beginning, not my end.
Some curled small body stirs in the quick
Frozen spot at the heart of atom and flame.

So many lives come, smoking and crashing over this coast —
Their births and deaths are my own.
They are broken by this double gift,
To break and keep, as the sea's struggle and fall
Fumbles back to marble ; the flux continues.

Fugue for Wind and Rain

WE come into a new time ; the heavy-mooned
Darkness hangs its orange crater flare
Above the sea.
My beaches are quiet : not a crab
Shuffles to disgorge its load of soft bulk from its outworn
Shell and die
In patterns on the sand. To-night
The wind sickens with heat : late strollers loaf
And stumble over kerbs ; and all
Earth's energy's coiled with this soaking sheet wrung
From the insomniac's dreamed sleep of the windstorm.

We come into a new time,
The world and myself : parable of the dog
Who buried his sense of smell with the bone-scraps,
And could find neither.
Consuls, lictors, slaves —
Dipped in Caesar's blood, blood of the fishes ;
Men and their knives of rule, manners, lives, hypocrisy
Of bride and groom, ride on
Bloodily to rebirths. In my effort to call them back
I make slaves of everything I see : that ditch
Where wineskin-fat cactuses gripped
The white solid fortress rock,
Where red-back beetles fought and tore at each other's
Strung nerves : in the violence of thunder off the hills'
One rainstorm in a month, —
In our bodies gored by the flame of July night.

Night along the sea promenade,
Black as my boots and finer than hair,
Drifts with the flickering torches of ships towards that far
White mustering of daybreak —
Time of the Greeks and before, the sea, these coasts

A haze of bound chapters now.
Over this nurturing ache of black
Nothing breaks ; but is made to know its final breakage plain
And whole as a part
Of the fissure it came from.   I look,
And can see no change : but am myself
The sign itself of change in everything : the clean, sharp
Fissure that bleeds the cactus, the deadly
Rote and scrabble of the red
Beetles spitting out their eggs . . .

Storm draw the water out of me.

This sea has many coasts,
And every inch and brown pool
Is a fingerprint.   The gannets come
Plunging, wreck their sight ; the sea-salt keeps
The crab-flesh it corrodes ; and the grape-
Avenging Dog-star locks
These fiery lives to the pillows we drown on.
Age has its lovers :
And neither history nor bad experience can ever redeem my one
Fault-finding
First error.   I look for the change of light, now
Over this sea : which to-morrow promises only by small chance
To reveal, be re-revealed
Through its weak heart of water, my body, my blood.

Third Time Lucky

TWICE I called, and twice
A surging upcrack wave bundled my voice
And all my belongings away out of earshot.
I stood alone in the sea,
Up to my neck in the swirl —
And called, not helplessly,
But as a man calls who has been denied
Too often to want his echo to obey ;
And rages with his head
Under the feeling pulse of stars,
To that emptiness where sounds break —

Rose, and clawed my way to the sand,
And a meal of crabs, fish-heads ; violence
Lying scattered and dead at my feet,
From the sea's last wave, barest returns.

The Birth of a Shark

WHAT had become of the young shark?
It was time for the ocean to move on.
Somehow, sheathed in the warm current
He'd lost his youthful bite, and fell
Shuddering among the feelers of kelp
And dragging weeds. His belly touched sand,
The shark ran aground on his shadow.

Shark-shape, he lay there.
But in the world above
Six white legs dangled, thrashing for the fun of it,
Fifty feet above the newborn shadow.

The shark nosed up to spy them out;
He rose slowly, a long grey feather
Slendering up through the dense air of the sea.
His eyes of bolted glass were fixed
On a roundness of sun and whetted flesh,
Glittering like stars above his small brain —

The shark rose gradually. He was half-grown,
About four feet: strength of a man's thigh
Wrapped in emery, his mouth a watery
Ash of brambles. As he rose
His shadow paled and entered the sand,
Dissolved, in the twinkling shoals of driftsand
Which his thrusting tail spawned.

This was the shark's birth in our world.

His grey parents had left him
Mysteriously and rapidly —
How else is a shark born?
They had bequeathed him the odour of blood,
And a sense half of anguish at being
Perpetually the forerunner of blood:

A desire to sleep in the currents fought
Against the strong enchaining links of hunger,
In shoals, or alone,
Cruising the white haze off Africa,
Bucked Gibraltar, rode into the Atlantic —
Diet of squid, pulps, a few sea-perch.

But what fish-sense the shark had
Died with his shadow. This commonplace
Of kicking legs he had never seen :
He was attracted. High above him
The sunsoaked heads were unaware of the shark —
He was something rising under their minds
You could not have told them about : grey thought
Beneath the fortnight's seaside spell —
A jagged effort to get at something painful.

He knew the path up was direct :
But the young shark was curious.
He dawdled awhile, circling like a bee
Above stems, cutting this new smell
From the water in shapes of fresh razors.
He wasn't even aware he would strike ;
That triggered last thrust was beyond his edgy
Power to choose or predict. This
Was carefully to be savoured first, as later
He'd get it, with expertise, and hit fast.

He knew he was alone.
He knew he could only snap off
A foot or a hand at a time —
And without fuss — for sharks and dogs
Do not like to share.
The taste for killing was not even pleasure to him.
And this was new :
This was not sea-flesh, but a kind
Of smoky scent of suntan oil and salt,

Hot blood and wet cloth. When he struck at it
He only grazed his snout,
And skulked away like a pickpocket —

Swerved, paused, turned on his side,
And cocked a round eye up at the dense
Thrashings of frightened spray his climb touched.

And the thrashing commotion moved
Fast as fire away, on the surface of sun.
The shark lay puzzling
In the calm water ten feet down,
As the top of his eye exploded above
Reef and sand, heading for the shallows.
Here was his time of choice —
Twisting, he thought himself round and round
In a slow circling of doubt,
Powerless to be shark, a spawned insult.

But while he was thinking, the sea ahead of him
Suddenly reddened ; and black
Shapes with snouts of blunted knives
Swarmed past him and struck
At the bladder of sunlight, snapping at it.
The shark was blinded —
His vision came to him,
Shred by piece, bone by bone
And fragments of bone. Instinctively
His jaws widened to take these crumbs
Of blood from the bigger, experienced jaws,
Whose aim lay in their twice-his-length
Trust in the body and shadow as one
Mouthful of mastery, speed, and blood —

He learned this, when they came for him ;
The young shark found his shadow again.
He learned his place among the weeds.

Monsoon

A SNAKE emptied itself into the grass.
A lizard wriggled out of a cup of ferns.
The pebbles, quiet, but nudging to follow the dust
Downwind, struggled with consciences,
Vaulting back as the gust, passing, kinked the long grass.
Then first we heard it, the long rush and rake
Abrading, stripping the earth's back, as the rain
Trailing its millions of wires, and voiding first
The lecture hall, the library and bungalows —
All the gardens springing taut, and the tennis courts
Smudged like wrecks at sea — the downpour came,
Caving its seething wall onto our verandahs,
Submerging the whole house.   And we froze,
Like water-spiders clenched in their sacs of breathing,
Crouched, dry and firm in the damp close mouth of the wind,
As the tropics snapped and tore at our moderate blood —

Then after an hour the ground steamed openly.
The rain, flickering northwards into the shallow hills
Left little puddles behind, rubies aflame
In the fattened grasses drinking the sunset down,
Deep, through stem and root, and into the cave of stone
Where the scorpion hungers, carrying his bruise down.

Donkey's Graveyard

BONES and bones.
But the skin is looser, cooler,
Coarse, flesh filled with wayfaring ants.

A tumbril carted the donkey away.
His wide mouth swallowing dirt
His hooves had silenced for ever.

But some maniac with a whip still tried
To get at him through the grass-tips —
In an effort to escape he lay perfectly still,
Ear-bladders choked, potato-split hooves.

Nothing had ever had so much time to watch.
Every free movement had seemed
A revolution, an anarchy —
Heresy along the rims of his eyes,
Practical disobedience in an uplifting kick.

But bats were the donkey's ears —
Who has seen the bones of a bat ?
At night, across the shrill tenement fronts,
Their flickering severe laughter controlled him —

And are antennae now. The switch ears,
The swiping tail : every extremity which took in
Whispers past that plumb stupor,
Or wasted the gestures his master paid for,
Killed by his length of life yellowing along his spine
Slowly, like caries,

Dragging the underworld with it.

But what was that nexus of feeling, heart,
Even the ants couldn't find.
Probably the skin, which is grass,
Or the jawbone-shaped soil,

Burning through the sun in flocks of soot,
And droplets of scalding sunlight.

The Black Oxen's Curved Back

WHERE is there true strength.
In my spine ?
Not in my head, or in my heart.

Can stamina come from sleep ?
My knuckles are tiny stones
That can be broken.

Over the grass the mosquito gobbles everything.
His proboscis firm, sharp
As an anaesthetist's needle.

I welcome him. Sting here ! Sting to the heart !

Groundhog

AT the tip of my gun the groundhog sits
Hunched in the sun a hundred yards away.
At this range my Hornet's steel-lipped
Bullet could bleed him dry as a star,
As a rag in the pitching drought-drugged field.

Grasses waver and hide. I watch
His shadow's hare, quick at its burrow's
Mouth ; the flinch of his rodent hump
Too far to see, like a piece of my eye put out.

No lead gift for a hawk this bead I draw.

Magnetic steel's the moment's only touch
Between us. Though his teeth and scent are sharp
They twitch no warning from the hot bright air.
And I cannot kill, but mark him, fat
As a neighbour safe in his rocking-chair.

Flat on my hips I lie in wait.
Earth beats with my heartbeat, and now
My body's jelly's hardened to take the blow
Of its triphammer weight at the soft exposed
Centre. Imagining it, I retreat —
Wait minutes as his black speck grows
Whiskering through the stalks of Indian corn
To confront me with 'Thou shalt not kill' —
A matter of temperament. No, his fate's
Inhuman, not mine. The riddle is why.

The riddle's this nerve that pecks at my hand.
Scissors to slice my aim's thread now would touch

39

Terror like a jumping nerve : Zero-urge,
Guiding my right hand and my eye —
Not the will's choice crying unmistakably No.

I fired because confusion made me think . . .

One spoilt instant's enough to be conqueror.

And now his brown blot melts to its darkest hole,
But I've beaten him there ; in the dark, I feel him drop
Slithering past me, wet at the spot I touched.

The Virtues

BUT to-day, walking by the sea
Among the ruptured orange-crates and dirty linen skin
Of the harbour, I watched a seagull land
Soft on a flank of timber to rest.
And if this is a soul, I thought,
Let him continue : for his heart is whole, and he falls
Neither under the knived
Wheels of women, nor
Lets his coiled intestine run to waste and rot
In the stink of harbours.
'Rest your fill !' I thought. And turned,
And saw a boy of maybe ten
Level a stone at its bobbing whiteness. The stone fell short,
As the boy will, and the man
After him will. So the quarrelsome heart, poised,
Chooses its target, blind to the depth
And breadth of chance beyond it. Man only learns
To aim better. Beside that fact
The bird's sheer, resting, clever
Whiteness on the water, paints
The sea a funeral black
For the heart's hopeful stones.

Cockroach and Star

THE sea rises at night,
The white-walled village submerged in the sea-wind.
A cockroach gazes at a star,
Its feelers meditating death.

Nightmares rise with the sea.
White walls make the peace of asylums.
Cockroach and star
Are each unfathomable —
They are not my contemporaries.

To kill the one and gaze at the other
Traduces ideas of time and space
No equation solves.   We're each his own
Night and nightmare toiling around one vine.

I look, and could have believed
All things my eyes held, gripped fast,
Were mine for life, without question.

I could have believed : but watch
The frantic energy of the dying cockroach
Feel towards a star which I thought
In rage my foot'd brought closer —
The average savage act of a man
Who by killing the small, achieves the great
By default ;   or thinks he does.

The whole night becomes that star.
In dreams the cockroach winds its milk-
White wound around my open mouth —
I roar, and darkness chokes the sound.

The Circle

THE spider hasn't dreamed about his
Place in history ; nor does the fly
Feel persecuted, churning around on its wings.

The spider's merely a grapple for his stomach ;
The fly, trawling in muck
Talks too much for its own good.

Even a butterfly, a mouse, or a small bird
Falls to the bigger species of spider —
Mechanical like tanks, patient as machine-guns ;

But the fly works no miracles.
Not like the ruly ant, or the self-
Sealed factory of a spider's nerves.

The naturalist has no allegiances : he watches
The beginning and end of the short, unequal tale
Again and again, until his notebook's filled ;

And at night, their scale small and intact,
The flies and spiders stream from his brain . . .

Entering his wife's dream, they eat her alive.

Bone-Patch

Now are the days to watch,
Mornings shuttered like the face ;
The body dissolves in smoke. Rich
Is the Fall like a flattered old queen,

Given to trick humours, to storms
That blaze like metal-cutters.
Eastward, the cold riveters begin
Drilling and blunting the sky's iron.

The bruised metal spreads, over my hands,
Across my face. Like a strip
Of dangerous cat my frozen eyes
Hunt, dilated.

And hunt back up the will's
Track, devouring scents
Some pemmican-hungry guide might
Overlook. In the brown forests

(Where fires have not charred) they seek
This one track in myself, the past
Engraved by a claw, adamant
Beneath black roots. And find

Suddenly, this patch of bones —
One arm crushed under it
Smashed like a thumb in a trap.
The flat skull bites at a stone,

Eyesockets double as flowerpots.
Squatting, I peer again ; discern
These shreds worm-free as ivory,
Angled like toothpicks in the bared

Gums of the forest moss.
I reflect : some human shape,
An eye, surely, appropriately flowers
Here, beyond its last risk

Of error. And here teeth gnaw
Some stony problem to death, that hours
Would not unwind in life, or leave
Moss-surrogates to finish. Look, —

The whole fits perfectly the parts. Yet
That crushed arm worries me ; and suddenly
I startle in the bones' shape this
Rabbit, trapped, frozen beneath its cry.

Remembrance Day

THESE tatters and drifting hands
Sifting in piles, along fences, at the roots
Of the maples, are pleaders.
Without causes, they're carried away by the rivers
To change character ; are
Brainwashed in billions, come swarming at you
Reminders of a lifetime's fragmentation.
Keep cool as the wind now.
No one is obliged to take these pessimists'
Captive advice to heart
Or head. I've made my peace
With all the seasons ; and autumn particularly,
Jamming the nerves' wires with its rusty static.
Make your peace too —
Frenzy is what the dead leaves sing
Long after the rain breeds order again,
And the snow hugs to breast what it cannot hold.
Leaves, pleaders, hands —
Always the earth voids itself back into earth,
And returns as earth ; comes back as prepared graves
Covering our once-ornamental lives.
Among all that's spawned and lives, only man and his gods
Die self-consciously enough to care.

Street Stroller

STRIDING too slowly to catch up with that glint of sun
Which might have held a Chinaman, a cat, or a butcher's
Work on a missing body, I know
Health comes with facing horror. I find
Dreams flesh me so closely my muscles become poisoned,
My body fitfully weak as the scene of a murder,
A disappearance, or an unknown animal . . .

Struck dead, this city's pavement spits out rain,
Unfamiliar as New York, or Phoenix. My bedsheets
No laundry would accept now, knowing my sleep —
Such unrest has no specific outside itself.
I have created my city in a minute's open hand.
Its eczema spreads, to infect my whole body.

Clean Break

ALL winter the thudding sparrows came and went,
Despoiling our bread-crumb sill. And I lay in a sweat,
Watching them peck out, bit by bit,
The fabulous plenty of my heart.

Imagining their worst plight, I thought my mind must break,
Imagining their budded claws, like scaffolding
Scrapping above the snow, and the bodies under the snow,
I lay, and could not dream ;

And could not think. My brain refused such food,
But only lay and stared, until the walls, returning
Like an eavesdropping squad of surgeons, hemmed me in ;
And I groped for signs of age, a first white hair . . .

Knowing, a man pays dearly who seldom thinks,
By having his thinking done for him ;
Which is about as pleasant a trait as
Being cuckolded.
           *   *   *

Now, in the warmth around me the rosebuds break alight ;
My flesh glows dense ; my arms, hooked like sickles
Encircle and clutch them ; bindweed, lupins, roots
Bitter as scammony, and the touch-me-not
Barbed squiggles of the centipedes' horned fingers.

All day the earth's on fire ; I burn
With the damp rheumatisms of the loam,

A dense hydrangea-head among the tougher skulls,
Feeling the leather-jackets nip under the grass,

Under the winds that jump the furrows and tracks,
Winnowing slowly like a thresher at half-speed ;

And lie, and gaze up at the sun where butter melts
Drop by drop on my hands, and stings, but heals.

Have Patience

SHEPHERD with no flock or crook,
Calling across the stones,
Innocence beyond our deepest recollection.
Something unsettled in the eye —
You could not call it a thought,
Hardly a feeling either.
Something dextrous in the smile's wrist,
As if the mouth was the whole
Body, not just an expression of it.

Only over this sparse ground,
Where the sun rolls marbles all day long
Until they fetch up against night —
A voice I had not heard before
Calling across the stones ;
My desultory nerves plucked
Like twigs, torn up dry through the skin ;
The upripped nerves of barren places —
And all around it this eye flat
Like an idiot's, innocent ; a lake
Tilting its level through me.

I Think I am Becoming Myself

THIS is life at the marrow,
No-telling and secretive. In this quiet month
All appearance has been merely figurative ;
Whatever I touch might prove the prime mover.

Patience is a tact due to time —
Old-fashioned and ungrateful. So my hands
Miss your plain body, every shape of limb
Grows huge exaggerated as eucalyptus'
Smooth wind-sucking dormant tension of sap.

If the tree should wilt and close up,
Under the dream and the dream's fantasy
And under that, in a detritus quicksand of blind
Thick wanting —
What ? There life is cold, adequate,
The order bland, the senses blunt as dead tools.

No, this is life at the core, time single.
Beyond this is just a waiting on dates : time
Told by clocks is not time of blood.
Bare objects attend and listen —
Our reunion will be slow and cautious and final.

Desperados

THESE four lie on a blanket,
A cluster of cactuses hides them from quick
Discovery and the road.   Three are grown men,
Fat and moustached, stretched flat on their backs with eyes
Wide and staring, as if the sun
And not bullets had struck them dead.
The fourth, a child, lies closest in the photograph,
Her eyes half-shut with the instantaneous
Headache of lead.   Now in this child's face
The crime folds its hands and waits —
Horror-struck.   While somewhere in those far hills,
Baked white as the whitest bread,
Black figures with smoking pistols break
A cigarette and share it.   Why did she die ?
They do not ask now.   They squat,
Hands slumped between their knees, waiting the outcry.
And it almost seems the photographer
Was the first one here :   his silver shutter and lens
Piercing through flies and the blood
Caked on the child's face, gouted on the men's chests.
She was the child of this fat
Official she fell beside ;   whose round, greedy stare
Somehow smuggled his life out through his wounds
Past the customs of death.   He looks surprised —
As if caught in a last act of graft —
And the child beside him, like a sick child,
His graft once protected.   Together now
Their tragedy speaks more shrilly than in life :
Her trust, and his shrewd lack of it
Which bought bullets for both on a dusty road ;
And the daughter entered her father's life
Without wincing . . . The other two don't count.
Their deaths enter the hills where the gunmen crouch.

Two Riders

LOOSE, tethered loose
This horse combs serenity with its eyes,
Though fly-troubled.
The bigger man dismounts,
Moves round the horse's rump into full shadow.
The smaller one basks under his broad hat,
Under the strong sun that wrinkles a desert horizon
And sets lizards thinking.

This scene I just imagine.
Why is it so important —
Why erase the hazardous energy of life with what's
Merely apparent in the mind —
This tethered horse, the two contradictory men,
Different in habit, endurance and build,
Circling the one animal heart ?

The men do not know me.
The horse in repose is companionable
Only in this moment of fatigue and trust.
The men must continually forgive each other
Their differences : they share this horse for ever.
Probably trusting the horse they trust each other.
They have only stopped to rest themselves
Briefly in my mind : they are welcome.

The world, as they pose now, cannot change them much ;
The true sun blacken or desert them
Beyond either's endurance.
The horse is all heart —,
Its resting heart goes pounding on like hooves
Any moment to gallop the desert to sweat on its back,
And be stabled at nightfall.

Between Seven and Eight

AMPLE the swallows threading above
The first sunlight on those white walls, and the black
Pitch church roof.
Too early yet, still half asleep,
Earth trembles at its most wide awake —
And the old are the first ones up,
Coughing on verandahs, waiting patiently for the sun
To touch their faces, and breed flies in their joints.

The old are quicker. For dawn
Is the slow beginning of the last time,
And their habit of sleep a memory, like everything else.
Hairs of dry grass rust on their hills,
Asses pump thick bleats through their blood
With an effort the heart cannot master now.

They will die, we will all die.
The earth is great with death.
This beginning to be quiet and alone is a preparation,
And a last dignity. These are the sun —
The black grandmothers stiff in their crushed cane,
Old widowers heavy with an overripeness of life,
Propped on corners, eyes squeezed shut at the sun
And flush of swallows, consciences, church-bells.

Seeing in the Dark

Now night falls. Though it was always night,
Has been since the last
Recollection of light closed its lids on that first
Curtaining of plankton in the sea.
It is deeper than night now. Look there —
Our eyes see shadows and shadows and shadows
Bundled untidily in the dark
Like last night's clothes. But these live,
While we live and die ; and being so heavy and loam-
Full of life, die gradually, with great
Clear conscious dying thoughts
That imagine our way for us,
As a hunting-pack does, hot muzzles of earth ;
That imagine our way ahead of us
With their powerful scenting hunger.
Death is this shutting of the rose of meat —
Its lips fastened, sewn together,
Lifeless and dumb as moth-dust.
Now begins the reckoning-up
Of its million lifetimes. What gift's your speech
Light, light — for this last time,
Light, for this hot last
Time of all times ? Your cord draws tight
Between the smack of the night-
Capsulating bullet, and the hard
Staying hand of a starved reason that works
Slowly ; that works well, and delivers
The black night
Eyes to see itself at the last, dead eyes or living.

The Crèche

THE crèche of faces, like wintering crocuses, lay mute
under their cauls of white wool. I stood at the extreme
end of the room, facing the wide fissured mirror, and tried
to identify one child that had its fingers twisted to a hard
ball in the rough smock of homespun the nuns had sewn him
into.

This one, I knew, was not pitted and scarred like the others,
but would have slept in a silksoft crib and blue initialled
sheets in the now heavily shelled château. The lamps, looking
like nuns' wimples, hung over the stark lines of cots, stiff
and crisp, starched cotton such as I'd dreamed of, feeling
the lice nip deep in my thick socks, touching tenderly the
crescent weal on my belly where the rat had clung scrabbling
with its claws.

His face, I sensed, would be free of scars and sores, something perhaps crying a little, softly, to itself, that its
guardians could not get at now to retrieve. In the glaring
silence of the fusty ward I could still, though barely, hear
the seventy-fives, and the bigger guns, one-five-fives and
naval guns, and the heavy soft flocculent heave of the mortar-
bursts. Looking more intently now, I realized there wasn't
time, that soon the tanks, the armoured cars, and the Taubes
would be circling the village, and an inky smoke would blot
up all daylight at the wire-barred windows of the room, making
further searches impractical.

So I shouted out my own name ; and the long cot lines froze
suddenly still, as if the first mortar shell had just now
snapped the roof. But nothing moved or spoke, or cried even,
and I saw that the nuns had gone away taking their clay jars
and crucifixes with them, out of the village. The face I was

searching for lay there, among the others, undiscoverable ; and sleeping, I imagined, but with its pink shocked mouth open wide on a high silent wailing that followed me, like the sharp tuning-forks of bullets striking the wires, as I stumbled out into the soft April mud, haunted and nameless, as before, belonging nowhere.

PRINTED IN GREAT BRITAIN BY
LOWE AND BRYDONE (PRINTERS) LIMITED, LONDON